The Blue Room

David Hare was born in Sussex in 1947. In 1970 his first play *Slag* was performed at the Hampstead Theatre Club. In 1993 three of his plays, *Racing Demon*, *Murmuring Judges* and *The Absence of War* were presented together in repertory at the Olivier Theatre in London. Since 1983, nine of his best-known plays, including *Plenty*, *The Secret Rapture*, *Skylight*, *The Judas Kiss*, *Amy's View* and *Via Dolorosa* have also been presented on Broadway.

DAVID HARE

The Blue Room

freely adapted from
ARTHUR SCHNITZLER'S
La Ronde

faber and faber

First published in 1998
by Faber and Faber Limited
3 Queen Square, London WC1N 3AU

Typeset by Faber and Faber Ltd
Printed in England by Mackays of Chatham PLC, Chatham, Kent

A CIP record for this book
is available from the British Library

ISBN 0-571-19788-4

2 4 6 8 10 9 7 5 3

Pour son anniversaire

Preface

It was never Schnitzler's intention that his loose series of sexual scenes, *Reigen*, should be publicly performed. When he wrote them in 1900, the author called them 'completely unprintable' and intended only that they should be 'read among friends'. It was no surprise when the eventual première of the work was closed down by the police in Vienna in 1921. Similarly, the actors in its first Berlin production the same year had to endure a six-day trial on charges of obscenity.

For years the sketches enjoyed an underground reputation. In 1923, when Schnitzler was sixty-one, a performance was given in a private house in London, again for friends only, with members of the Bloomsbury group joining cheerfully in the proceedings. Virginia Woolf was moved to complain in a letter that 'the audience felt simply as if a real copulation were going on in the room and tried to talk to drown the very realistic groans made by Partridge! It was a great relief when Marjorie sang hymns.'

It was only when Max Ophüls made his famous film in 1950 that the work escaped its provocative reputation and became associated instead with a certain kind of enchantment. The film, set in turn-of-the-century Vienna, brings out all the wistfulness and elegance of the subject matter. It boasts one of the most formidable casts in French cinema with Gerard Philipe, Danielle Darrieux, Jean-Louis Barrault and Simone Signoret appearing, among others. Few people knew the original work well enough to notice that Ophüls had, in fact, adapted the text with extreme freedom, even introducing a figure –

not in Schnitzler – of the all-seeing ringmaster, superbly played by Anton Walbrook. ('What am I in the story? I am in short any of you. I am the incarnation of your desire to know everything.')

After the success of the film, the play became better known as *La Ronde*. For myself, I first heard of it when my father told me that only when I was grown up would he allow me to see what he called his favourite film of all time. Since 1981, when the theatrical rights fell temporarily out of copyright, there have been a good many stage versions, and in many different languages. Some of them choose, as *The Blue Room* does, to re-set the play in a contemporary world. Mine is also not the first version to allocate the ten parts to just two actors.

Over the years audiences have continued to argue about whether the idea of the sexual daisy-chain that is at the centre of Schnitzler's conception is profound or over-neat. Whichever, it is wonderfully malleable. When I have put plays by Chekhov, Brecht and Pirandello into English, I have never considered anything but a fairly strict fidelity to the original. But when Sam Mendes asked me to adapt Schnitzler, I instinctively chose to follow Ophüls's example, licensed by the knowledge that the author himself never put the material into a form where he foresaw it being performed.

The hundred years that have followed the writing of *Reigen* have seen a supposed upheaval both in social attitudes and in sexual morals. But the fascination of the work is that its treatment seems hardly dated at all. Schnitzler was not only Freud's almost exact contemporary. He was also, like Freud, like Chekhov, a doctor. His essential subject is the gulf between what we imagine, what we remember and what we actually experience. You have to wait years (in fact for Marcel Proust to stop partygoing and get on with his great novel) before you find a European author having the prescience to chart this treacherous, twentieth-century territory of projection and desire with as much longing and insight as Schnitzler.

David Hare
July 1998

Characters

The Girl (Irene)
The Cab Driver (Fred)
The Au Pair (Marie)
The Student (Anton)
The Married Woman (Emma)
The Politician (Charles)
The Model (Kelly)
The Playwright (Robert)
The Actress
The Aristocrat (Malcolm)

*The play is set in one of the great cities of the
world, in the present day.*

The Blue Room was first performed at the Donmar Warehouse, London, on 10 September 1998 with the following cast:

The Girl
The Au Pair
The Married Woman   } Nicole Kidman
The Model
The Actress

The Cab Driver
The Student
The Politician   } Iain Glen
The Playwright
The Aristocrat

Directed by Sam Mendes
Designed by Mark Thompson
Lighting by Hugh Vanstone
Music by Paddy Cunneen
Literal translation by Julian Hammond

Darkness. Music. You have the impression of the stage opening up, as if it were expanding. You begin to see a Girl, sitting on a bench, smoking a cigarette. As the stage grows around her, it becomes clear she is under a scrubby tree by the side of a street. She looks eighteen, like an amateur, in a short black leather skirt and shoes, but she also has an odd self-confidence. A Cab Driver walks past, taking no notice. She makes no reaction. Then, ten seconds later, he passes again, going back in the other direction. This time, the music stops and she speaks as he passes her.

Girl What? What did you say?

Cab Driver I didn't say anything.

Girl I thought you said something.

Cab Driver No.

Girl What made me think you just spoke? (*She puts out her cigarette.*) Do you want to come home with me?

Cab Driver Do I want to go home with you? Go *home*? Why would I go home with you?

The Girl is impassive, not responding.

Where is your home?

Girl Quite near.

Cab Driver Where?

Girl South of the river.

Cab Driver I'm not going south.

Girl We can take a taxi.

Cab Driver *Take* a taxi? I drive a fucking taxi.

Girl Is it yours?

Cab Driver It's mine.

Girl I mean, does it belong to you?

The Cab Driver turns to go.

So?

Cab Driver I haven't got any money. I just spent the lot on sushi.

Girl So?

The Cab Driver looks at her a moment, recognizing her.

Cab Driver Great. Let's go.

Girl And suddenly we're in a rush.

Cab Driver How far is this place of yours?

Girl It's ten minutes by cab.

Cab Driver Oh look, forget it. Ten minutes? No. Forget it. I have to work. I've made nothing tonight. And I'm not doing it in the car. It's the first rule of driving. I never do it in the car.

Girl Give me a kiss.

Cab Driver Here?

The Girl takes his hand and leads him quickly to a darker place across the street.

Girl Now give me a kiss.

She kisses him. It's magical, suspended for a moment. They stay in each other's arms. It is dark in the street and deserted.

The kiss is the best bit. I like the kiss best.

Cab Driver It's still too far.

The Cab Driver looks at her. They start to walk towards the river. As they go down by the riverside, it is very beautiful, the reflection of the water thrown high against the wall.

Girl What do you think? Do you think you'll always want to drive a cab?

Cab Driver Shall we just stick to what we're doing?

The Girl throws a glance at him.

Girl What I want . . . what I really need is someone long-term. I need someone ambitious.

Cab Driver Long-term I'd make you jealous.

Girl Oh yeah?

Cab Driver Sure.

Girl Why?

Cab Driver I'm irresistible. Women can't resist me.

Girl Watch out. It's dark down here. One foot wrong and you're in the river.

Cab Driver I'd love to be in the river.

The Girl smiles. He tries to push her up against the wall.

Girl Let's do it on the bench.

Cab Driver I'm not walking that far.

The bench is about three feet away.

Let's do it here.

Girl Watch out, or we'll both be in the water . . .

Cab Driver Great . . .

Girl Wait. We'll both be in the water.

Music engulfs them. The lights go out.

☙

Light returns. The Girl is lying on the ground. The Cab Driver is kneeling beside her, his hands on his knees.

Girl It would have been better on the bench.

Cab Driver On the bench. Off the bench. Up the fucking wall. What's the difference? Up you get.

Girl Hey, where you going?

Cab Driver Back to work. (*Suddenly he reaches down with unexpected tenderness and pulls her up. He smiles.*) I told you. I've done no business tonight. (*He begins to leave.*)

Girl What's your name?

Cab Driver Oh no, I'm not telling you my name.

Girl My name's Irene.

Cab Driver Irene, well!

Girl What's yours?

They both smile. The Cab Driver turns to go.

Hey, listen . . .

Cab Driver What?

Girl Come on.

4

Cab Driver What? What are you asking?

Girl Come on. I didn't want any money. Really. I didn't. But, please, give me some money.

The Cab Driver looks at her a moment.

Cab Driver It went on the sushi. I'm not an idiot, Irene.

The Cab Driver goes.

Girl Wanker! Fucking wanker!

2. THE CAB DRIVER AND THE AU PAIR

At once the sound of Elvis Presley. A slow ballad is being amplified very loudly and resonantly inside a neon-lit dance hall. Suddenly a door opens. Warm-coloured light falls across a darkened space and on to the Cab Driver, who is already in the room. In the doorway stands the Au Pair. She is young, with a foreign accent, and is wearing a dress which is subtly too small for her. They are in the middle of a disagreement.

Au Pair I don't want. I really don't want.

Cab Driver Why not? Why not?

Au Pair We were dancing.

Cab Driver Come in the room. Just for a while. It's an interesting room.

The Au Pair moves into the room, leaving the door open.

Au Pair Do you know my name? Can you even my name remember?

Cab Driver Can I your name what?

Au Pair Ah, the verb . . .

Cab Driver The verb?

Au Pair Yes. In my country the verb comes last.

Cab Driver Not in ours.

Au Pair No.

Cab Driver We get on with it. (*He looks her in the eye.*)

Tell me, then. If it's so important.

Au Pair Marie. And you?

Cab Driver Fred.

Au Pair I can't call you Fred.

Cab Driver Why not?

He closes the door. Pitch dark. The Au Pair giggles.

Au Pair It's so dark. My God, look how dark it is.

Cab Driver You'll be all right. Whatever happens you'll be all right. Girls say they're scared, but what are they scared of?

Au Pair The dark. They're scared of the dark.

The Cab Driver lights a match and makes a big arc with it.

Cab Driver This way, my dear.

The Au Pair smiles, slightly charmed. He lights a cigarette with the match, then pulls at a string above his head. A bare light bulb comes on. We are in a dusty store-room. Cardboard boxes, not much else.

Why not tonight? Just tell me, why not?

Au Pair Because.

Cab Driver Girls all say 'because'. I don't know what 'because' means.

Au Pair It means because.

Cab Driver Because it's Tuesday? Because it's been raining?

Au Pair Just because.

Cab Driver Because you don't fancy me? It's hardly likely, is it?

Au Pair Why not?

Cab Driver Well, just look at me.

Au Pair It's so dark I can't see you.

Cab Driver So it can't be that then, can it?

The Au Pair looks away, not responding.

What's the problem? I promise you, I won't tell anyone.

Au Pair Oh, that's great. That's a real come-on . . .

Cab Driver What's wrong with that?

Au Pair That makes me feel really sexy. What a great line! 'I won't tell anyone'!

Cab Driver Well, no one'll know.

The Au Pair throws a sideways glance at him.

Au Pair I saw you looking . . .

Cab Driver What do you mean?

Au Pair More with the blonde than with me you danced.

Cab Driver Which blonde is that?

Au Pair The one that like a frog looks.

Cab Driver Oh yeah, well, that one. She's an old friend. Of a friend. So is that the reason?

Au Pair No.

Cab Driver So do you want to go back?

The Au Pair looks at him for a second.

Au Pair Not yet.

It's a concession. The Cab Driver cheers up.

Cab Driver Do you like the music?

Au Pair I do. I like it very much.

Cab Driver Elvis.

The Au Pair stops. She is quiet.

Au Pair What do you think the reason is? Why should I risk? That's the reason. Because it's not safe any more. I'll only risk if . . .

Cab Driver If what?

Au Pair If it means something. If I'm to risk, it has to mean something.

The Cab Driver takes her in his arms and they kiss. But she pulls away.

So?

The Cab Driver doesn't reply for a moment or two.

Cab Driver It means something. I promise.

Au Pair Does it? Does it really mean something?

They go down together on a bed of cardboard boxes, which crush beneath them. He pulls again at the light string.

It's not . . . for Christ's sake . . . it's not . . . oh God, it's not . . .

From the darkness, the sound of the Cab Driver, supremely happy.

Cab Driver Yes, oh yes! Oh yes, oh fucking yes!

Au Pair I can't see your face.

Cab Driver What's my face got to do with it?

Au Pair Let me see your face.

Music engulfs them.

9

Near dark. A streak of ambient light hits only the Cab Driver. The two of them are still where they were.

Cab Driver Well, there we are. (*He seems content.*) We can't lie in boxes all night.

He lights a match for a cigarette, which they share. We can't see the Au Pair's face. The cigarette glows in the dark.

It's got so bad, I heard there was this prisoner on death row. They asked him, 'Any last request?' He said, 'A cigarette.' They said, 'You're on public property. It's against the law.'

The Au Pair stretches, ignoring his story.

Au Pair Oh God.

Cab Driver Oh God, what?

Au Pair *Tu es un animal.*

Cab Driver That's right.

The Au Pair turns and looks at him.

Au Pair Fred . . .

Cab Driver What? What, Fred?

Au Pair Tell me . . . tell me what you feel.

Cab Driver What I feel?

Au Pair Yes.

Cab Driver I've just shown you what I feel.

There is a pause.

Au Pair Frederick, tell me. Put into words.

Cab Driver You know what I feel.

Au Pair Then kiss me.

The Cab Driver stops and kisses her. The sound of Elvis grows again in the distance. It's romantic. Then he breaks.

Cab Driver Imagine. He's about to fry, and they still won't give him a fag.

He gets up and pulls at the light string. She is looking at him from the floor.

Au Pair Help me up.

Cab Driver Come on, then.

He pulls her up to her feet. The Au Pair stands, adjusting her clothing.

What are we going to do? Are we going back to the dance?

Au Pair If you like.

Cab Driver I don't know. I'm sort of confused. To be honest, you've sort of confused me.

Au Pair Have I? How did I do that?

Cab Driver I don't know. If I knew, then I wouldn't be confused. (*He takes a step away.*)

Au Pair Well, I have to go.

Cab Driver What?

Au Pair Yes. I have to get back. I'm treated like a servant. By the whole family. I have the cats to feed, the dogs, the humans. I'm a slave.

The Cab Driver frowns, lost.

Cab Driver How are you going to get home?

Au Pair I'll walk.

Cab Driver You can't walk. It's dangerous. At this time of night. Don't you want a lift?

Au Pair (*shrugs*) If you like.

The Cab Driver stops, suddenly raising his voice.

Cab Driver I don't get it. What am I meant to say? What do you want me to say? I'm offering you a fucking lift.

The Au Pair smiles and makes to go. He follows her, better humoured.

And what does that mean? What does the smile mean?

She smiles at him again.

I'd like a dance. Can we have one more dance, please? I mean, if we don't, isn't it just a bit brutal?

She looks at him.

Au Pair Yes, Fred.

The sound of the music grows. The Cab Driver closes his eyes and starts moving his hips.

Cab Driver Don't you just love that bit? Don't you just love it? (*He's in a world of his own. He points towards the lone chair in the room.*) Look, sit down. I'll get us a beer. We can dance in here.

Au Pair I don't have long.

Cab Driver I won't be long. (*He opens the door. The crowded room glows with colour and warmth.*) Don't you go now.

Au Pair I won't.

Cab Driver Well, don't.

He turns uncertainly and goes into the dance hall. The Au Pair sits alone.

3. THE AU PAIR AND THE STUDENT

The kitchen of a modern house in a well-off area of town. It is modishly decorated with stainless-steel hooks from which hangs a faultless batterie de cuisine. *There are grey venetian blinds on the gleaming windows. At a big butchers' block table in the centre of the room the Au Pair is sitting in a blue blouse and slacks and stunning blue slippers, writing a letter. It is plainly very hot. After a few moments the Student appears at the kitchen door. He has a book in his hand. He is in fashionable jeans and a T-shirt. He is extremely nervous.*

Student What are you doing?

Au Pair Writing a letter.

Student I see. Who to?

Au Pair A man I met at a dance.

   The Student does not move.

Student It's so hot. It's so unbelievably hot. It's never this hot at this time of year. There's nobody left in town. Am I the only person still working? They didn't take you to the country?

Au Pair No. (*She has stopped writing, but has not moved from the table.*)

Student What's coolest? Vodka? Do we have vodka?

Au Pair We ran out. Your father drank the lot.

Student It's him insisted I read law. It's a family tradition.

Au Pair The drinking?

Student The law. (*He does not acknowledge the joke.*) It's all right, I'll just have some water.

Au Pair There's the tap.

Student Can you get me a glass?

It is clear he expects the Au Pair to do it for him. She gets up, gets a glass from the cupboard, then goes to the tap and turns it on. They are both running with sweat.

Let the water run, so it's really cool.

The water overflows from the glass into the sink. The Au Pair keeps it running.

Who called?

Au Pair I'm sorry?

Student I heard the bell ring.

Au Pair Did you? When?

Student Earlier.

Au Pair When?

Student This morning. I've been up there so long I lose all track of time. I was expecting a friend.

Au Pair No friend. Here.

She has taken the glass across to him and puts it in the Student's hand. Their hands touch.

Student Thank you. I'll take it upstairs.

He goes out. The Au Pair goes to the mirror and adjusts her clothing, improving the line of her breasts against the shirt. She pours herself a glass of water. Before she can turn, the phone rings. She answers it.

14

Au Pair Yes? You want another one? (*There is a slight pause.*) No. You come down.

She drinks her own glass of water. Then gets a third glass from the cupboard and pours a fresh glass. As she finishes, the Student appears at the door, without the book.

Student Thank you. So, excellent. You're enjoying it here? You get on with my father?

Au Pair Very well.

Student My mother likes you. You relate to my mother. Which is always important. I've found.

Au Pair Here.

Student She's an interesting woman, don't you think?

Au Pair Who?

Student My mother.

The Au Pair hands him the fresh glass and their hands touch once more.

Thank you.

He takes it and the Au Pair moves away.

Do we do things differently here?

She doesn't answer.

Come here, Marie.

Au Pair Sir.

Student Not sir. Nobody's called sir any more. God, I hate that idea. Those days are gone.

Au Pair Sir? (*She has moved closer to him.*)

Student Please. I just wanted . . . I was looking at the shirt. Considering you . . . I know you have no money.

Or we pay you so little, rather. And you have such nice things. Can I see it? Please? (*He takes the lining between finger and thumb.*)

Au Pair What's wrong with it?

Student Nothing. It's the most beautiful blue.

Au Pair Sir?

Student I mean it. I'm telling the truth.

He puts his arm round the Au Pair's waist and draws her to him. She leans back as he unbuttons her blouse a little and kisses her chest.

Your skin is beautiful. It's white.

Au Pair Now that's just flattery.

Student Nothing wrong with flattery, is there?

Au Pair No. Flattery is no harm. (*She sighs under his kisses.*)

Student What a beautiful sound . . .

Au Pair Sir . . .

The Student has suddenly dropped to her feet, still nervous.

Student And what beautiful shoes. Blue as well. What do you call them? Indigo?

Au Pair Cobalt.

Student Are they . . . I mean, what I'm asking, do you get them from the same shop? (*He wraps himself round her knees.*)

Au Pair Sir, if the doorbell rings . . .

Student The bell won't ring.

Au Pair At least close the shutters.

The Student goes across and pulls the blinds. The hot afternoon light slats through from outside, their faces in darkness. He looks at her from across the room.

Student Why are you shy?

Au Pair You think I'm shy?

Student Anyone who looks like you has no reason to be embarrassed. If I looked like you, I wouldn't be shy. If I smelt like you.

There is a pause. Neither of them move.

The other evening, the bathroom door wasn't closed. You'd fallen asleep in the bath.

They look at each other, not moving.

Au Pair I'm ashamed.

Student I've seen you already. I'm half-way there, I'm already half-way there . . .

He moves quickly across and pushes the Au Pair decisively on to the butcher's block. Then he climbs on top of her. He starts to pull her skirt up, clambering over her.

Au Pair What if the bell rings, what if your friend comes . . .

Student My friend won't come . . .

Au Pair What if he does?

Student Let him ring. Don't go to the door. Just leave him. Don't go to the door.

Au Pair What if he comes? What if your friend comes?

Student He won't come . . .

17

Music engulfs them. Darkness.

The music stops. The doorbell rings insistently. It is still dark. You sense they are lying side by side.

Student Shit!

Au Pair What?

Student How long has it been ringing?

Au Pair It's only just started.

Student How do you know?

Au Pair I was listening.

It rings again.

Student Can you go?

Au Pair What?

Student Go and look through the letterbox. It may just be a beggar.

Au Pair You're joking.

Student I'm telling you: go and take a look.

The Au Pair pulls down her skirt and goes out. The Student pulls up his trousers and opens the blinds. The light is liquid now, yellow. The Au Pair returns.

Au Pair Whoever it was, they've gone.

Student Are you sure?

Au Pair Of course I'm sure.

Student Do you think it was my friend?

He seems restless. The Au Pair doesn't notice and moves towards him again.

Au Pair Well, we'll just never know.

The Student looks down.

Student I'm going to get a coffee.

Au Pair Why?

Student I think I'd better go. I think I'd better be going.
I'm going to the café.

The Au Pair just looks at him.

I mean it. If my friend calls . . .

Au Pair He won't call . . .

Student If my friend does call . . .

Au Pair He won't.

There is a pause. The Student is quite angry.

Student If he does. I am saying, Marie, if he does . . . *if* he
does, please tell him where I am. Which will be in the
café. (*He pauses a moment.*) I mean, if you could do your
job.

Au Pair Sir.

4. THE STUDENT AND THE MARRIED WOMAN

The Student's bedroom. It is evening. A classic student tip,
the walls maroon and festooned with posters of rock
stars. The bed is covered in garish, disorderly sheets.
There are books, records, discarded clothes, a dartboard.
The Student comes in, throwing down a load of books
and a plastic bag, tearing off his clothes, grabbing a clean
shirt and a pair of trousers. He stuffs his discarded clothes
under the bed. From the plastic bag, he takes out a bottle
of cognac, and a foil-wrapped container, which he opens.
Inside are a selection of frozen hors d'oeuvres – vol au
vents, little meatballs, prawns on sticks. He fussily moves
them around on the little tray to make them look more
impressive, then sets them down beside the cognac. He
takes a swig from the bottle.

As he does so, the doorbell rings outside. He goes to the
bedroom door, opens it, listens. Someone has got to it
before him. So he sits down in a chair with a book, trying
to look casual. The Married Woman comes in. In her
early thirties, she has tried to disguise her arrival by wear-
ing extremely tight trousers, a big shapeless coat, a scarf
wrapped round her head and dark glasses. She looks like
a cross between Jackie Onassis and the Invisible Man. She
stands a moment with her left hand on her heart, as if
mastering an overwhelming emotion.

Married Woman My God!

Student I know. I'm sorry.

Married Woman That was terrifying.

Student I know.

He gets up to move towards the Married Woman, but she presses herself with her back to the door.

Married Woman I never want to do that again.

Student I know.

The Married Woman stands, recovering.

Married Woman I thought . . .

Student So did I . . .

Married Woman If I came, your house would be empty. You promised.

Student Yes. I didn't think. The au pair. (*He takes a step towards her.*) It's all right, I know for a fact she doesn't read the papers.

Married Woman I should hope not.

Student She doesn't know who you are.

Married Woman I came straight from work. You have no idea . . .

Student No . . .

Married Woman When I said . . . when I agreed . . . I wanted to see where you lived . . .

Student Here it is.

Married Woman I just wanted to see where you lived.

Student Here it is.

The Married Woman is at the door. She has not moved.

Here it is. Well at least sit down, won't you?

Married Woman I can stay five minutes.

She moves quickly across the room. The Student clears

the chair of assorted student garbage, and cleans it
quickly with his hand. She sits. He frowns slightly.

Student The problem is, I can't actually see you . . .

Married Woman What?

Student I mean with the glasses.

Married Woman Ah. (*She takes her glasses off.*)

Student And the scarf.

But rather than take it off, the Married Woman gets up,
still nervous.

Married Woman Is this your room?

Student It is.

Married Woman Is this where you work? I shan't come
again. (*She turns, suddenly.*) It's so hot! It's so bloody hot
in here!

Student I'll take off your scarf.

He takes off her scarf. The Married Woman does not
resist.

Married Woman What's wrong?

Student It's the first time we've ever been alone.

He inclines his head to kiss her but the Married Woman
moves a step away.

Married Woman You asked me to visit you. I'm visiting.
You simply don't understand . . .

Student No . . .

Married Woman The press in this country . . .

Student Oh, the press, yes . . .

22

Married Woman They have no values. They have no respect.

The Student frowns, murmuring assent.

Student Disgusting.

Married Woman It's so ridiculously hot in here!

Student That's because you've got your coat on.

Married Woman Then take it off.

The Student comes round behind her and unbuttons her coat. He takes it to put it on the chair with her other things.

And now I must go.

Student Emma!

Married Woman I mean it. I really do mean it. I'm friends with your parents, for God's sake.

Student So?

Married Woman We go ski-ing together.

The Student looks at her a moment.

Student Do you want a brandy?

Married Woman Yes. But get me some water first.

Student I'm sorry?

Married Woman A glass of water. You do have a kitchen, don't you?

Student Yes. (*He hasn't moved.*) Have a brandy instead.

The Married Woman watches as he pours cognac into a toothmug.

Married Woman I thought I could do it and I can't.

23

Student Why? Isn't this what we want? We're together. We're in a room. For once without your husband's eyes boring into us . . . (*At once he retracts.*) All right, sorry, I shouldn't have mentioned him . . .

Married Woman You aren't married. You understand nothing.

The Student gives her the brandy.

I was coming up the stairs, I saw myself . . .

Student Emma, I know how unhappy you are.

Married Woman Do you?

Student I know your husband's world. Politics! My God! How could anyone be happy . . . someone of your intelligence, your sensibility . . . how could you be happy in a world of presentation and lies? (*He is suddenly angry.*) What do you think this is? Some squalid assignation?

The Married Woman looks at him directly.

Married Woman What is it, then?

Student This is love. (*He nods slightly at his own admission.*) Jesus. I mean, this is it. It's love. I'm in fucking love. I can't live without you. It's true. Maybe I sound naive. Well, I am. I am naive.

The Married Woman has taken a vol au vent from the foil container.

Life's not a rehearsal. We're only here once.

Married Woman And how many women have you said that to?

Student Well, none. At least since I met you.

Married Woman Ah well, that's something.

They both smile.

Anton, you promised . . .

Student What did I promise? What did I promise exactly?

There is a pause.

Married Woman Take off my clothes.

The Student fumbles a moment.

Student Let me just . . . how does this . . .

Married Woman Let me do it, all right?

He gets off the bed. The Married Woman is wearing a body stocking under her clothes.

Student What are you wearing?

Married Woman It's a body stocking. Madonna wears them. (*She gets into the bed in the body stocking.*) My God, it's cold in here.

Student It'll warm up pretty quickly.

Married Woman Well that's rather up to you, isn't it?

The Student, undressing, is disturbed by this remark and addresses us directly.

Student She shouldn't have said that.

The Married Woman has undressed under the sheets.

Married Woman Come, come to bed, Anton . . .

Student I'm coming . . .

Married Woman There's a smell of honey . . .

The Student gets into the bed, taking her in his arms.

Student It's you. It's you who smells of honey . . .

Music engulfs them. Darkness.

៖

Silence. The Married Woman is sitting at the side of the room. The Student is still in bed.

Student It's my fault. I'm sorry. It's all my fault. I knew this would happen. I could tell. I knew it was wrong. Emma? Emma?

The Married Woman does not reply.

I read an article.

Married Woman An article?

Student Some of the most famous men in history have had this particular experience.

Married Woman Ah.

Student Churchill. Regardless. Julius Caesar.

The Married Woman is frowning slightly.

I'm not saying it makes me feel better. It doesn't. As you say, it doesn't matter, but even so.

Married Woman No. Though to be fair, you did promise me you wouldn't do anything and you've stuck to your promise . . .

Student Emma . . .

Married Woman This man is as good as his word!

Student That isn't funny.

Married Woman No one can say you didn't warn me.

Student What is this? Is this some sort of joke?

Married Woman No, for goodness' sake. It's just . . . do we have to be so bloody serious?

Student No, of course not.

Married Woman I didn't think it happened with young men, that's all. I thought it happened with clapped-out older men. Or men who haven't got any shagging left in them.

The Student frowns, trying to ignore this sudden vulgarity.

Student Another thing, I tell you, I met this stockbroker. He'd had to wait fifteen years for the woman he loved – she was married, or something. And when they did finally get to be together, they just lay side by side. For six whole nights, they did nothing. They just cried.

Married Woman Both of them?

Student They cried for joy.

Married Woman Do you think that's true of all stockbrokers, or just this one, because . . .

Student What is this?

Married Woman I think I may avoid stockbrokers in future. If all they can offer is communal weeping.

The Student suddenly raises his voice.

Student Honestly, this whole thing seems to have cheered you up in some way . . .

Married Woman Not at all . . .

Student In some obscure way, you seem in very good spirits.

Married Woman I'm not.

Student I thought women were meant to reassure men on these occasions.

Married Woman Are they?

Student I thought they were meant to put it lightly aside and make them feel better.

Married Woman So?

Student I'm feeling worse.

Married Woman Look, it's fine. We're friends. We're – what's that word? – comrades.

Student Oh, for God's sake!

Married Woman You said it first. You said it! 'Let's be comrades,' you said . . .

Student Did I?

Married Woman I couldn't believe it. I'd never met any-one who used that word seriously. (*She suddenly changes tack.*) And now I have to go . . .

Student Emma, please . . .

Married Woman I have to!

Student Just stay five minutes. Please!

Married Woman All right, but only . . . only if . . . you make me a promise.

Student What promise?

Married Woman Trust me.

There is a pause.

Student What do I do?

Married Woman Trust me. I know more than you. Lie completely still.

The Student lies back. She stands at the end of the bed.

That's it. If you move, then I leave. Just lie. Lie.

*She stands above him, about to solve the problem.
Music engulfs them. Darkness.*

❧

Darkness. Silence.

Married Woman Oh, my beautiful boy . . . (*She turns on
the light.*) What time is it?

Student (*looking at his watch*) Eight.

Married Woman Eight, my God! (*She wraps the sheet
round herself and starts urgently to gather up her things.*)
I know it. I just know it.

Student Know what?

Married Woman Tonight. Tonight will be the night when
for once he comes home early. Where are my shoes?

*The Student has got out of bed and holds out her
shoes.*

Student Here.

Married Woman You don't get it, do you? You don't
understand. This could be the end for the both of us.

Student Why?

Married Woman Because I'm a hopeless liar, that's why.
I'm hopeless!

Student Then you'll just have to get better.

Married Woman And all this for you, for a man like you.
Here, give me a kiss.

*They embrace, she holding her clothes, then she runs
into the bathroom, very happy.*

A hopeless liar, and hopelessly shy.

She closes the door. The Student starts to pull on some trousers, then stops and goes to eat several hors d'oeuvres. She speaks from inside the bathroom.

(*off*) Anton!

Student Yes?

Married Woman (*off*) Thank God we didn't just cry.

The Student smiles contentedly.

(*off*) How will it be? When I see you across a room one day?

Student What do you mean, one day? We're meant to be at the rally tomorrow.

Married Woman (*off*) What rally?

Student We're all going. Your husband's speaking at the rally.

Married Woman (*off*) I won't go. Are you mad? (*She reappears. She grabs at some hors d'oeuvres as she finishes dressing.*) I couldn't possibly. I'd never survive.

Student I'll see you tomorrow.

Married Woman It's out of the question.

Student Then the day after. Get here by six.

Married Woman Can I get a cab on the street?

Student Sure. It's a deal. The day after tomorrow. You'll be here at six.

Married Woman There's no deal. We'll discuss it tomorrow. At the rally.

The Student embraces her.

Student My angel!

Married Woman Be careful of my hair.

Student Tomorrow politics, then, next day, love.

Married Woman Goodbye.

Student (*suddenly worried*) What . . . I mean, I'm just asking: what *will* you tell him?

Married Woman Don't ask. Don't even ask.

The Student kisses her for a last time. She goes. He is left alone. He sits down on the sofa and eats some more hors d'oeuvres.

Student I'm fucking a married woman.

A wealthy bedroom. The Married Woman is lying in bed, working on papers. There are two single beds. Above them, some modern paintings. The Politician, early forties, comes into the room, his tie loose round his neck, and his sleeves rolled up. He looks tired. The Married Woman does not look up.

Married Woman Have you stopped already?

Politician I'm exhausted.

Married Woman You never stop before one.

Politician The government of the country . . . (*He smiles, self-satirising.*) Besides, I felt lonely.

Married Woman Oh really?

The Politician puts his hand in front of her eyes.

Politician Don't read any more. You'll hurt your eyes.

The Married Woman does not move.

Is this how you thought it would be? When you married me?

Married Woman I had no idea.

Politician For some time now, I've wanted to talk to you, Emma. To thank you, really.

Married Woman Thank me?

Politician Yes. For your forbearance. I know there are times when I'm close to you, and times when I'm not.

Sometimes, I just have to take one step back. I have to withdraw . . .

Married Woman Yes . . .

Politician It's because of the work . . .

Married Woman I'm sure.

Politician It's purely my work. The irregular hours. The separations. (*He gestures towards his single bed.*) But, on the other hand, there is a compensation.

Married Woman What's that?

Politician These moments when we find each other again. (*He sits on her bed.*) I remember someone saying to me years ago: a real marriage is always moving. It's never still. At any one moment you're either moving closer together or moving further apart.

Married Woman Which at the moment?

Politician Oh, closer. (*There's a moment's pause.*) I was remembering how we started . . .

Married Woman Ah, yes . . .

Politician How things were at the beginning. If we'd gone on like that, we would have both gone mad.

Married Woman Would we?

Politician Of course. If we'd gone on as we started in Venice . . .

Married Woman Venice!

Politician Yes. My God! (*He moves a little closer to her.*) If we'd gone on like that for . . .

Married Woman Months, you mean?

Politician Yes.

33

Married Woman Instead of weeks?

Politician Exactly. I think we'd have gone up in flames.

Married Woman Perhaps.

The Politician shakes his head at the narrow escape.

Politician I don't know. I've watched so many marriages conceived in bed, lived out in bed, and, let's face it, finished off in bed, everything over in a space of a few years . . .

Married Woman Yes . . .

Politician Bed the only criterion, bed the only place of contact, bed the only thing holding things together . . .

Married Woman Yes . . .

Politician Thank God ours isn't like that.

There is a moment's pause.

Married Woman No.

Politician You have to be friends, don't you? Friends as well as lovers. You know what I think's important? What's most important of all?

Married Woman No.

Politician A sense of humour.

Married Woman Ah.

Politician If you can laugh together, as we laugh together . . .

Married Woman Sure.

Politician . . . then there's a basis. Then there's something solid. A woman you can laugh with.

Married Woman Is that what I am?

Politician Among other things, yes. (*He looks at her fondly.*)

Married Woman Are you coming to bed?

Politician I am. (*He kisses her on the forehead and then gets up. He takes three identical little mobile phones from his pockets and sets them down in a row on the sideboard, like hairbrushes. Then starts to change.*) It's quite frightening, you know, in my work. I look back. I belong to a generation that valued freedom above everything. Yet it's as if people have forgotten what freedom entails.

Married Woman Have they?

Politician Personal liberation was such a wonderful idea, but here we are, thirty years later, and governments have to deal with the consequences . . . (*He takes off his shoes and socks.*) Social disintegration, homelessness, cities falling apart, social services overstretched. I heard of a young woman the other day, five children by five different fathers. And behaving as if somehow that's her God-given right. And the rest of us have to care for those children! (*He stands in his boxer shorts.*) Oh yes, freedom's a wonderful thing, but I sometimes think you should have to pass a test to prove you deserve it.

Married Woman And do you deserve it?

Politician Well, I think I probably do, yes.

Married Woman Goodness.

They both smile.

Politician Seriously, you and I have the money . . .

Married Woman Ah, yes . . .

Politician Well, it's a factor. It does make a difference. We can care for our children, we can look after them, we can bring them up without burdening society.

Married Woman So. Freedom's a question of money?

Politician Not entirely. (*He smiles again, confident.*)

Married Woman The funny thing is, you tell me so little about your own past . . .

Politician Me?

Married Woman Yes.

Politician Do I?

Married Woman About your own freedom, I mean.

Politician I must change. (*He goes out to the bathroom.*)

Married Woman It's so strange, we've been together eight years and in those years have you ever talked to me about what your life was like before?

Politician (*off*) Of course I have.

Married Woman But, I mean, really talked?

The Politician returns, in pyjamas.

Politician You know all the names . . .

Married Woman Of course . . .

Politician The list. Haven't we been through the list? Who I was close to.

Married Woman But the *kind* of life. I know very little.

Politician It's not a life I want to think about. (*He gets into his bed.*) I'm so much happier now.

Married Woman Are you?

Politician Of course. (*He shakes his head, appalled at his*

36

memories.) My God, all that confusion, all that uncertainty . . .

Married Woman Were there so many then?

Politician You've asked me this before. Why does it matter?

Married Woman It matters. I want to know. Tell me.

Politician Does it? Does the past matter? (*He pauses a moment, reluctant to go on.*) Emma, you've lived a sheltered life . . . (*He smiles as if to anticipate.*) Compared with me at least, let's say compared with me, so the point is, most of us know, there's a certain kind of woman . . .

Married Woman Is there?

Politician Of course. You know what I'm saying. It's not – what's the phrase? It's not *politically correct* – but in their hearts everyone knows there are two kinds of women . . .

Married Woman Two?

Politician Only you're not meant to say so. And I am someone who spent many years of my life – too many perhaps – with that first kind of woman.

Married Woman And what kind of woman is that?

Politician Oh, come on, do I really need to spell it out?

The Married Woman just looks at him, not answering. He's provoked.

The kind of woman you just sleep with.

She makes no reaction.

Well, look . . .

Married Woman I see . . .

Politician It's fine when you're young . . .

37

Married Woman Of course . . .

Politician When you're young, it's natural. It's part of growing up. But it's not . . . look, it's not a life. It's not a life like we have. With children.

Married Woman I want more children.

Politician Well, good. (*He waits a moment.*)

Married Woman What's happened to the women?

Politician Why?

Married Woman Are you still in touch?

Politician Of course not. Don't be ridiculous. Do you think now that I'm married . . . do you think I wouldn't have told you?

Married Woman Well . . .

Politician I tell you everything. (*He looks her straight in the eye.*) Both sides understand. In that kind of relationship, to be crude, you both know what's going on. It's not for ever. That's not what the whole thing's about.

Married Woman No?

Politician No, it's just for passing, just for passing . . .

Married Woman Pleasure.

Politician Yes. Just for passing pleasure. Mere pleasure.

Married Woman Yes.

Politician Infatuation.

Married Woman Yes.

There's a pause. She looks at him.

Come here.

He smiles and gets in beside her.

Politician And I dread to think . . . truly I dread to think what has happened to one or two of them. These were not happy souls. Some of them couldn't even hold down jobs.

Married Woman I see.

The Politician shakes his head slightly at the memory.

Did you sleep with married women?

Politician What?

Married Woman Did you sleep with married women?

Politician Emma, I never broke up a marriage.

Married Woman Ah . . .

Politician Now that is something quite other. I'm sorry but that is something quite different.

The Married Woman looks at him a moment.

Married Woman You think so?

Politician Of course. It's a basic principle. Everyone has the right to follow their own . . . wotdyumcallems, their own needs, their own desires, but they have no right to destroy other people's happiness. Isn't that right?

Married Woman I don't know.

The Politician is frowning.

Politician You don't sound sure.

Married Woman No.

Politician Is that because you have friends who do it? Do some of your friends sleep with married men?

Married Woman I think so.

39

Politician And what do they feel?

Married Woman I don't know.

Politician How do they defend it?

The Married Woman shrugs slightly.

Married Woman I don't think they have to *defend* it.

Politician How do they live with all the lying, the deceit? The sheer level of organization. Being where you shouldn't be, at times that don't fit! The danger, the strain. And for what? Just that one extra moment of happiness. That one short moment of bliss.

Married Woman Hmm. (*There's a pause.*) Are you sure you never did it yourself?

The Politician hesitates.

Politician Look, if I tell you, truly, it's the saddest memory I have.

Married Woman Go on.

Politician A woman I knew when I was young.

There's a silence.

Married Woman She was married.

Politician Yes.

Married Woman How long did you know her?

Politician Long enough.

Married Woman I see.

Politician Some months.

Married Woman Did you love her very much?

Politician Can a man love a liar?

There's another silence.

Married Woman And where is she now?

Politician Oh . . .

Married Woman No, tell me.

Politician Do you want me to tell you?

Married Woman Yes.

Politician She died. (*He is thoughtful now.*) Not happily. Unhappily. In unhappy circumstances. She died in a godawful mess of drink and obsession. Which is, to be honest, what I knew would happen. I feared it. There was something tragic in her. Something not right.

The Married Woman is watching him hard.

Married Woman What are you saying? That her death was some sort of judgement?

Politician Oh no . . .

Married Woman That it was because of who she was? Because of what she did?

Politician No. I would never say that.

Married Woman What was her name?

Politician Estelle.

Married Woman Estelle.

They are both thinking a moment.

Politician But I have only known real love once. And that is with you. (*He reaches and takes her in his arms.*) Let me kiss you.

They kiss.

Married Woman Charlie . . .

Politician I feel so safe in your arms, so happy.

Married Woman Do you?

Politician If only we'd met when I was younger. I would never have needed to know anyone else. You're a beautiful woman, you hear me? Beautiful . . .

He turns the light out. Music engulfs them. Darkness.

❧

The music stops. They are lying in each other's arms.

Married Woman You know what I'm thinking of?

Politician No.

Married Woman Of Venice.

Politician Ah yes.

Married Woman Of our first night together.

Politician Yes. (*There is a pause.*) What is it? Tell me.

Married Woman If all our nights could be like that. If you could always love me like that.

Politician Yes. (*There is a pause.*)

Married Woman Hmm.

Politician What's wonderful about marriage: that there will be time for everything. I mean, not everyone has Venice, even as a memory.

Married Woman No.

They lie, both awake.

Politician Goodnight, my darling.

Married Woman Goodnight.

6. THE POLITICIAN AND THE MODEL

A room in The Metropole. It is a desperately fashionable minimalist hotel, pared away to essential surfaces of marble and glass: a high-class knocking shop. The Politician is sitting back with a cigar contentedly on the sofa, having finished a lavish dinner. With him is the Model. She looks about seventeen, in a micro-skirt and skinny jumper. She is spooning at a chocolate ice-cream in a pretentiously large glass. The television is in her eyeline, and is playing with the sound turned down. The Politician watches her.

Politician How is it?

Model It's great.

Politician Can I get you another? You've no wine left. Here.

He pours her another glass. The Model drinks it straight down.

And now I'd like a kiss.

She kisses him on the sofa, then turns back to her ice.

Model You must think I'm a slut.

Politician Why?

Model Coming straight to the room.

Politician I don't think you're a slut. (*He tries to pull her towards him.*)

Model Hey!

Politician That wasn't the first time I'd seen you.

43

Model I guessed that.

Politician We could have gone for a walk first. If that would have made things more respectable.

Model Had you been following me?

Politician I'm not telling you anything.

Model Plenty of men do.

Politician I'm sure.

Model I never speak to any of them.

Politician No? You spoke to me.

Model And are you complaining?

The Politician kisses her violently.

Politician You taste of pudding.

Model I just have sweet lips.

Politician Really? Have men told you that before?

Model Some.

Politician How many?

Model I'm not saying.

Politician I want to know. It's important. I want to know.

Model Guess.

Politician Fifty?

The Model breaks away.

Model Fifty? Why don't you just make it five hundred? Fifty!

Politician I'm sorry. It was a guess.

Model Guess again.

Politician Five.

Model I am seventeen, you know. I'm not a total innocent.

She goes back to her ice. The Politician frowns slightly.

Politician You are desperately thin, my dear.

Model If you're a model, you have to look awful. That's the job.

Politician I can't believe you've got that quite right.

Model You have to look sort of awful but sort of beautiful as well.

Politician It's a balance, you mean?

Model Beautiful underneath.

Politician What does your boyfriend think? You must have a boyfriend. An attractive girl like you.

Model Why are you asking? Why do you want to know?

The Politician hesitates, phrasing it carefully.

Politician It's simple. I find myself . . . powerfully attracted to you.

The Model looks at him a moment, then gets coke out of her handbag.

Model Do you want some?

Politician No, thank you.

The Model empties it on to a little mirror. The Politician looks a little nervous.

Who was he then?

Model Who?

Politician Your last boyfriend.

Model Are you still on that? (*She looks up at him for a moment from preparing her coke.*) He looked like you. As it happens.

Politician Really?

Model Yes. Very like you, in fact. (*She goes back to her preparations.*)

Politician If you say so.

Model You talk like him, too. 'If you say so.' And you have the same way of looking.

Politician What way is that?

Model The way you're looking now. (*She looks up at him again.*) Don't. Don't look at me like that.

The Politician moves across and takes her in his arms, kissing her passionately. It's suddenly electric. Then she breaks free.

I'm going to go after this.

Politician Why?

Model Because I've got to get home, obviously. What will my mum say?

Politician You still live with your mother?

Model We came over together. There's five of us kids.

Politician What does your mother say when you don't come home?

Model She's out most nights herself. I'm the one who's working.

Politician Ah, well then . . .

Model I've got sisters still at school.

Politician And how old are they?

Model There's one who's thirteen. The other day I caught her out on a date. I couldn't believe it. The little slut!

Politician What did you do?

Model I beat the shit out of her when she got home. (*She sniffs a line of coke.*) That's what I'm saying. If I don't give them some discipline, who does? (*She snorts a second line.*)

Politician The strange thing is, you remind me of someone, too.

Model Do I? (*She sits back, luxuriating, closing her eyes.*) Who do I remind you of?

Politician Someone I knew when I was young.

The Model is quiet. Her eyes are still closed.

Model You haven't told me your name.

Politician Charles.

Model (*laughs*) Are you really called Charles?

Politician Why? Was that his name as well?

There is a silence.

You still haven't told me who he was.

Model He was a cunt. He was a cunt, or why else would he have left me?

Politician You were in love?

The Model is silent.

I thought your eyes were green, but they're blue really.

Model And isn't blue good enough for you?

47

The Politician takes this as a cue. He moves to kiss her.
But before he can she holds out her hand which is full
of pills.

Here. Take one of these.

Politician Which one?

Model A white one.

The Politician pops one in his mouth.

Two.

He takes both. Then, to amuse her, takes another at
random.

Politician Anything you say.

They kiss.

When did you meet this man?

Model I can't remember. I can't remember anything. The
room's going round.

Politician Hold on to me. Hold on tight.

The Model's eyes are closed. He slips to the floor,
putting his head between her legs.

How is that? Is that good?

Model I don't know what you're doing. (*She leans back.*)
God knows where it came from. It was the usual guy. And
he'd got it from some other guy. And he said. And he said.
He said he'd got it from another guy . . .

The Model puts her head back as music engulfs them.
Darkness.

ã€°

Light creeps back. The Politician is sitting at a desk in his

*rousers and shirt, very alert. The Model is lying on the
ofa, abandoned like a dish-cloth and, contrastingly, sleepy.*

Model Why are you so far away? Why don't you come
ere?

*The Politician turns and looks at her. He is plainly dis-
turbed.*

*esus, where did I get that stuff?

Politician Good question.

Model I would never have done it . . .

Politician Ah, that's very flattering, I must say. It was the
oke, was it?

*Suddenly the Model protests with a real, shocking vehe-
mence.*

Model I don't do this! I don't fucking do this! I don't
leep with men I don't know.

Politician Of course you don't. I know you don't. I can
ee that.

Model It's not me. It's not what I do.

Politician Well, that's good. I mean, that's good from all
oints of view. (He shifts, a little uncomfortable.) That's
what I was asking earlier, why I wanted to know. Who
lse . . .

Model Oh God, are you still going on about that?

Politician I'm just asking.

Model What for? *(There's a pause.)* What have I done?
Have I done something wrong?

Politician No. On the contrary. In fact . . . I was hoping I
might see you again.

Model Oh yes?

Politician Maybe not here. Maybe in some sort of place I might find for you.

The Model looks at him a moment.

Model You're married, aren't you?

Politician What makes you say that?

Model That's just how it looks.

Politician Would it bother you if I were?

Model What do you do?

Politician I'm a politician. I help run the country.

Model Uh-huh. (*Her gaze doesn't waver.*)

Politician Would it worry you? If it turned out you'd been with a married man?

Model Why should it worry me?

Politician That you'd helped him cheat on his wife.

Model Well, I'm sure she cheats on you.

The Politician laughs.

Politician Hardly.

Model What makes you so sure?

Politician I really don't think it's very likely.

Model Don't you? If she's anything like the women I know, then . . .

Politician You know nothing. You know *fuck nothing*! *You know absolutely nothing at all*! (*He has suddenly shouted at her. He gets up, very disturbed.*)

Model I thought you said you weren't married.

Politician Whether I'm married or not, you plainly know nothing about . . . about another kind of world to your own.

There's a silence while he recovers.

Model I didn't know you were married. I was just talking, all right? I was just talking.

Politician My fault. I'm unused to the pills. (*He goes over and sits beside her on the sofa.*) Listen, I need to see you again.

Model Do you?

Politician Of course. But for me, it's not easy. If we come to an arrangement. I have to say, in the nature of things I can't be watching you.

Model I don't suppose you can.

Politician I can't be checking up all the time. (*He looks at her a moment.*) I'm not talking about the moral side of things. That doesn't bother me. And, for myself, I shall have to be careful, meaning discreet. The press in this country is a scandal. It's completely out of control. But beyond that what I'm talking about is something else. (*There's a pause.*) The world as it now is. As it has become. I'll be frank. I'm talking about hygiene.

The Model looks at him in silence.

That's not unreasonable.

Model Ah.

Politician I can get us a place. It could even be a place where you lived. If you wanted to live by yourself. (*He smiles.*) Next time we'll be somewhere else.

Model Maybe.

Politician Where we can't be disturbed.

Model Maybe.

The Politician looks at her from across the room.

Politician Kelly, I'm offering you a life of your own. Independence.

The Model doesn't reply.

Isn't that what women want?

7. THE MODEL AND THE PLAYWRIGHT

A studio in a bohemian part of town, self-consciously artistic, full of books and CDs. A large modern writing desk is covered with papers and scripts. There is a piano at the back of the room. The curtains are drawn and the room is half dark. The Playwright opens the door, letting the Model in behind him. He is in his early thirties, rather intense. She is tottering on high heels, and a little bit the worse for wear.

Model Oh, this is lovely. It's beautiful. But I can't see a thing.

Playwright Your eyes'll get used to it. Your beautiful eyes. (*He kisses them in the darkness.*)

Model Hmm. My beautiful eyes won't have time to get used to it. I'm off in a mo.

  The Playwright ignores this remark.

Playwright Let's have candles shall we? There was a power cut a few years ago, and afterwards I thought: why go back to electricity? Everything is cast in a magical light. (*He has lit a candelabra, and now looks round, pleased with the effect. He gestures towards the sofa.*) Sit down over there. Sleep if you want to.

Model I'm not tired. Are you going to play the song?

Playwright Well, I am. It's a song of my own.

Model Of your own? I thought you were a journalist.

Playwright My God! What made you think that?

The Model has taken her coat off and slumped on to the sofa. He has sat down at the piano stool, displeased.

Model You said . . .

Playwright Jesus!

Model At the party you said you were a writer. Aren't journalists writers?

Playwright Hardly. I mean, generically, perhaps. Like rats are animals.

The Model nods at his desk with its swish computer.

Model Is that what your computer's for?

Playwright Oh yes, but I never use it. To me the feel of the pen on the paper is all-important.

Model Huh. (*She waits a moment.*) You said you were going to play me this song you'd written.

Playwright Did I say I'd written it?

Model Yeah, you did actually.

Playwright Did I write it? No. I helped write it, that's more accurate. Does it matter? No. Ultimately, is author-ship important? Come on, it's the work we should value, not the writer.

The Model doesn't reply.

Do you have any idea what I'm talking about?

Model About?

Playwright You didn't understand a word, did you?

Model Yeah.

The Playwright smiles contentedly.

54

Playwright How is it? Is it comfortable there?

Model Aren't you going to play the song?

Playwright Try to stop me. (*He sits down at the piano.*)

Blue, like blue like blue is how I'm feeling
Blew like how the wind blew all night long
And blew aside your cotton dress revealing
This, the opening of the opening of a song

You, like how you seemed at our first meeting
But are people ever truly what they seem?
For soon I felt that subtle, slight retreating
That marks the ending of the ending of a dream

I'm in the blue room
I'm in the blue
The dream was just a dream
It wasn't you

Hitch a passage to the moon on some Apollo
Get out and take a look at what you find
The earth looks kind of circular and hollow
And blue's the shade you'll see you've left behind

Blue, not pink, not red, not terracotta
But navy, royal, azure, all those hues
For if from space you look at us we're notta
Ball. We're a swirling, brilliant, cloudy mass of blues

I'm in the blue room
I'm in the blue
The dream was just a dream
It wasn't you

Tell me why this lonely feeling hits me

That the person who I wanted wasn't you
And let me say, if politesse permits me
That I'm left with nothing save the colour blue.

At the end the Model applauds, delighted.

Model It's great.

Playwright Thank you.

Model I mean, it really is great. (*She frowns slightly.*) What sort of writer are you?

Playwright Do you really not know who I am?

Model No.

Playwright This is wonderful.

Model Why?

Playwright I mean, I love the idea. Are you serious?

Model Of course.

Playwright Do you mean . . . you really don't recognize me, do you?

Model No.

Playwright Very good. (*He thinks about it a moment, pleased.*) What sort of writer am I? Yes, well, this is a very good question. This is something people have argued about. The work's not easy to put in a box.

Model Ah.

Playwright The work's won prizes.

Model The work has?

Playwright Well, I mean, I have.

The Model frowns again.

Model Do you have any drugs?

Playwright Drugs? I've run out. I write about them, of course. They're one of my defining subjects. But at the moment, no.

Model My bra hurts.

Playwright Take off your bra. Take anything off. It won't bother me.

Model Thanks.

She slips her bra off from under her jumper as he goes on talking.

Playwright Inevitably I get labelled, as if I'm part of a movement. They call me a post-romantic. I know. It's just a shallow name the press dreamt up. (*He thinks a moment.*) Restlessness. Longing. These things don't go away just because of what we call progress. We still search. We still pursue the idea. We land. We cast off. With luck, we make waves. But finally we have no control of the tide. (*He is lost in thought. He turns.*) What did I say?

Model What?

Playwright What did I just say?

Model Something about restlessness. Longing.

Playwright That's right.

Model 'No control of the tide.'

The Playwright has reached for a scrap of paper on the table and is making a note.

Playwright 'Control of the tide.' Good. (*He puts his note-book aside.*) Do you want something to drink?

Model I'd prefer something to eat. I'm starving. People think modelling's just swanning up and down.

Playwright That's interesting. Where do you live?

Model I've got a flat. Near the centre.

Playwright The centre? Really?

Model Someone . . . someone found it for me.

The Playwright is very close. The candelabra on the piano throws their faces into shadow.

Playwright You're blushing. It's dark. But I can tell you're blushing.

He puts his hand up to her cheek. The Model does not resist.

Tell me more about yourself. Everything about you interests me. Have you ever been in love? (*He stops her before she answers.*) Don't tell me. Let me guess.

Model I was engaged.

Playwright And you miss him, don't you?

There's a pause. The Model is beginning to cry.

Oh, I love it, I love it. Say something else. I'll take you away, I promise. Have you been to India?

Model No.

Playwright Let's go. We'll go to the Rajasthan. There are forts – can you imagine? – built over the cities. I'll put you on the battlements, and we'll fuck each other's brains out. (*He goes to collect the candelabra.*)

Model I wish I understood you. I wish I knew what you were saying.

Playwright That I want to be with you. That I can't get enough of you. That everything about you . . . your beautiful little jumper . . . (*He puts the candelabra on the floor* *beside the sofa and starts kissing her breasts through the material.*) Your naive untutored little skirt . . . and the thought of the paper-thin, onion-skin, fragile yellow papyrus of your knickers . . .

Model What?

Playwright I'm known for my enormous vocabulary. My capacious vocabulary! The egregious, rapacious, dithyrambic immensity of my individual lexicon . . . (*He suddenly raises his voice.*) Big words! My work is throbbing with big words! Trouser-bulging with polysyllables! (*He reaches down and starts blowing out the candles.*) We'll go. We'll go together to Jaipur.

Model Where?

Playwright I worship you. I fucking worship you, my child.

He reaches down and blows out the last candle. Music engulfs them. Darkness.

❧

The music fades. Voices from the darkness.

Playwright That was wonderful.

Model Oh, Robert . . .

Playwright And only now shall I tell you my name. (*There is a pause.*) I'm Robert Phethean.

Model Phethean?

Playwright Yes. I knew you'd guessed. I could tell.

Model I hadn't guessed. Really. I've never heard of you.

Playwright Are you serious? Do you never go to the theatre?

Model My aunt took me to *The Phantom of the Opera*.

Playwright I said the *theatre*.

Model I've never been asked.

Playwright Well, I shall ask you.

Model Great. But I only like funny things.

Playwright Do you mean comedy?

Model Or scary things.

Playwright Why's that? Have you never been to a proper play? A serious play, I mean.

Model What's the point?

Playwright Not even if it were by me? (*He gets up in the darkness from the sofa.*) I want to see you. I haven't seen you since we made love.

> He strikes a match to light a candle. She lies, unembarrassed.

Model Give me the cover.

Playwright In a moment. (*He pulls back the cover from her naked body and stands over her, candle in hand.*) You are so beautiful. You're what I've been looking for. Total natural naked innocence.

Model Ow! The wax is dripping. That bloody well hurts.

Playwright I'm sorry.

> The Model covers herself up again.

At first I didn't believe you. That you didn't know who I was. So many people . . . well, let's just say, without being arrogant, it's a big problem for me. People want to know me for the wrong reasons.

Model What reasons?

Playwright Wanting to sleep with me because of who I am.

Model Oh, I see.

Playwright Just hoping I'll put them in my work. (*He laughs.*) You really didn't know I was Robert Phethean?

Model I told you, I've never heard of you.

Playwright Ah, fame, fame! (*He shakes his head in ironic sadness.*) Fine, forget I'm a writer. Honestly. I'll be a shop assistant. I'll be a venture capitalist, if you like.

Model I'm totally fucked. What are you talking about?

Playwright Our future.

Model What future?

Playwright Let's just go, don't you think so? Do you have a few weeks?

Model Of course not.

Playwright Go and live in the woods. In the depth of the forest. It's what I've always wanted. Get away from all this. And then one day . . . just look each other in the eye and say goodbye.

Model Goodbye? Why? Why say goodbye?

Playwright Because you're too much for me. (*He takes her once more in his arms, wrapped in the cover.*)

Model I'm cold. Hold me.

The Playwright kisses her and looks at her kindly.

Playwright It's time we got dressed. I promise. I won't look.

He goes to the window. The Model starts to dress.

Tell me, would you call yourself happy?

Model Now?

Playwright In general.

Model I'm not unhappy.

Playwright I'm not asking about your circumstances or even the men in your life. What I'm asking is: do you feel alive? Do you feel you're really living?

Model You don't have a comb, do you?

Playwright I do. (*He picks one up from the table and moves across to give it to her.*) You look astonishing.

Model Thank you.

They are both still a moment, then she combs her hair.

Playwright It's not nine yet. Why don't we eat?

Model It'll have to be quick.

Playwright I'll get you a ticket for my play.

Model Do. (*She finishes combing, then turns towards him in the candlelight.*) I'm ready.

Playwright I'm looking at you and I'm thinking: if it could be like this. If it could always be like this.

The Model looks down, overwhelmed. He holds out an arm towards the door.

After you.

8. THE PLAYWRIGHT AND THE ACTRESS

A room in a country hotel, in rustic style. There is a large old-fashioned bed at the centre of the room and the dark walls are dimly seen to be hung with pictures. The room is dominated by a large window which is open. A huge net curtain billows and blows. At once the Playwright comes in carrying the Actress's luggage. She is magnificent, in her early forties, and splendidly assured. He puts the bag down and clicks vainly at the light-switch.

Playwright Oh, I don't believe it. The light doesn't work. Never mind. Look! There's a moon . . .

The Actress has gone to the open window and dropped to her knees in front of the moon. The Playwright closes the door.

What's wrong?

The Actress doesn't reply. The Playwright goes over and joins her.

What on earth are you doing?

Actress What do you think I'm doing? I'm praying.

Playwright I had no idea.

Actress I'm not a bloody heathen like you.

Playwright Goodness.

Actress Come and kneel beside me, infidel. It'll do you good.

The Playwright kneels and puts his arm round her.

Oh, sex, sex, sex . . . (*She gets up.*) And who do you think
I was praying to?

Playwright Well, to God, I imagine.

Actress That's just where you're wrong. I was praying to
you.

Playwright Then why were you looking out of the window

Actress What on earth are we doing? Where have you
dragged me off to, you blatant seducer?

Playwright It was your idea. 'The country!' you kept sayin,

Actress Well, wasn't I right?

Playwright Of course. It's beautiful. Only an hour out of
town and it's as if we're in paradise.

Actress It's bliss. You could write wonderful things here i
you had any talent.

*The Playwright frowns, swallowing this insult as she
goes and sits on the edge of the bed.*

Playwright Have you been here before?

Actress Been here? I lived here.

Playwright Really? Who with?

Actress With Fritz. With the magical Fritz. I adored him.

Playwright Yes, so you said.

Actress Oh, I'm sorry. Please, if I'm boring you, I'll go
somewhere else.

Playwright How could you bore me? I've never been less
bored by anyone in my life. As long as you don't talk
about Fritz. Let's make a rule. No Fritz.

Actress Well. Fritz was an episode.

Playwright I'm glad you can see that.

The Actress looks at him a moment.

Actress Come over and kiss me.

They kiss.

Playwright You're going to laugh when I say this but I find in you a kind of total natural naked innocence. I mean it.

Actress You do talk more bollocks per square metre than any man I've ever met. And now goodnight.

Playwright What do you mean?

Actress I'm off to bed. Can I have my bag, please? It's over there. (*She takes out a little Madonna and puts it on the bedside table.*)

Playwright And who's that?

Actress It's Our Lady. She's always with me. (*She smiles at him unkindly.*) And now thank you, Robert. Goodnight.

Playwright Goodnight?

Actress I've booked another room for you.

Playwright Another room? What do you mean 'another room'?

Actress Another room! This is like your dialogue. Everything repeated. 'Another room?' Yes. I've booked another room.

Playwright What for?

Actress To sleep in.

Playwright What is this?

Actress What is it? It's me wanting to change.

Playwright Change? Is this modesty? For God's sake you were in that play . . .

Actress Don't talk about it!

Playwright You were stark naked for an hour and a half. I personally saw the play three times.

Actress That's different. It's easier on stage. (*She suddenly raises her voice.*) Are you totally insensitive? Turn.

The Playwright turns to face the wall.

Playwright Perhaps I'll go for a walk. That always inspires me. I get all my best ideas at night. And knowing you're close, knowing my inspiration is near . . .

Actress You do talk like a prick.

Playwright Most women would say I talked . . . like a poet.

Actress Yes, well. Turn back. (*She has got into bed.*) Now you can sit on the side of the bed and tell me a story.

Playwright What sort of story do you want?

Actress Like . . . who you're being unfaithful to right now?

Playwright I'm not being unfaithful. Right now.

Actress I don't see why not. I am.

Playwright Well, that doesn't surprise me.

Actress And who do you think is the lucky man?

Playwright I haven't the slightest idea.

Actress Guess.

Playwright In the way of things, I suppose inevitably your producer.

Actress What do you think I am? Some sort of chorus girl?

Playwright Sorry.

Actress Guess again.

Playwright I don't know. The leading man. Benno.

Actress Benno? Do you know nothing? Benno lives with a postman.

Playwright Good Lord.

Actress He's the most married man I've ever met. (*She smiles.*) Can I make a suggestion? Robert, just get into bed.

Playwright That's what I wanted.

Actress And just get on with it.

Playwright Well, that's what I've been saying! (*He is undressing quickly.*) Listen!

Actress What?

Playwright The crickets are chirping.

Actress Don't be ridiculous. There are no crickets round here.

Playwright But you can hear them!

Actress Are we going to listen to non-existent crickets all night?

  The Playwright gets into bed with her.

Now just lie still.

Playwright What are you doing?

Actress Can I ask you something? Are you thinking of having an affair with me?

Playwright What on earth makes you think that?

Actress A lot of men want an affair with me.

Playwright Yes, but right now, I'm in pole position.

Actress Come on then, cricket. From now on, I shall call you cricket.

Playwright Cricket's good by me.

The Actress takes him in her arms.

Actress Talk to me. Tell me, come on, who do you think I'm betraying?

Playwright It's a pretty good bet you're betraying me for a start.

Actress (*laughs*) You're nuts.

Playwright Somewhere perhaps there's a man you haven't met. A man who waits and is perfect.

Actress Cricket, you do talk bollocks.

Playwright But if you met him, then you'd stop searching. And if you stopped searching . . . well, if you stopped searching, then you wouldn't be you . . .

Darkness. Music engulfs them.

❧

The music stops.

Actress Well, you have to admit that's a lot better than acting in damn stupid plays.

Playwright In my view, you act in rather good plays.

Actress Meaning yours?

Playwright Well . . .

But the Actress interrupts him, suddenly sincere.

Actress I agree. Since you mention it, it is a great play.

Playwright Thank you.

Actress You write brilliant plays.

Playwright Thank you.

A slight pause.

Actress God sees what we do. I shall confess you tomorrow.

The Playwright looks at her a moment, puzzled.

Playwright By the way, why did you skip that performance on Thursday? The doctor said you were fine.

Actress I did it to annoy you.

Playwright Annoy me? Why?

Actress Because you're conceited.

Playwright Me?

Actress You have no idea how everyone at the theatre hates you.

Playwright They hate me?

Actress Of course! Behind your back. They all say you're conceited. I'm the only person who defends you. I tell them you've a lot to be conceited about.

Playwright And what do they say to that?

Actress What do they say? What do they say? Who cares what the little people say?

Playwright Well . . .

Actress You know what the theatre's like. A low drizzle of persistent complaint.

The Playwright frowns, unhappy.

Playwright I've always found the writers above all that.

Actress Oh, writers!

The Playwright shifts, uncomfortable.

Playwright When you were saying . . . when you were saying about God . . .

Actress Yes?

Playwright What I'm asking is: is there a problem? For you? Does this create a problem?

Actress Why are you asking?

Playwright Well . . .

Actress What does it matter? You're not a Catholic.

Playwright I'm just asking. I'm interested.

Actress Don't even speak of it. You can never understand. (*She nods.*) Yes, wild in the dark, and then the guilt.

Playwright Even in love? Even when it's love?

Actress How often is it love?

Playwright Fritz, I suppose.

Actress Fritz was special. You, you're a whim. (*She smiles, ignoring his hurt.*) Still suffering from the chirping are you?

Playwright Non-stop. Can't you hear it?

Actress What you can hear is frogs, darling.

Playwright Balls. Frogs croak.

Actress Well of course they *croak*.

Playwright And that is not croaking, it's chirping.

Actress You are so bloody pigheaded. Give me a kiss, frog.

They kiss.

Happy now, frog? (*She laughs.*) Anyway, you've said nothing about my performance.

Playwright When I heard you'd been off, I just assumed you'd be a bit creaky when you got back. So I didn't bother.

Actress Creaky? I was brilliant!

Playwright Brilliant?

Actress People had to be carried out of the theatre.

Playwright You saw them, did you? They had stretchers, did they?

Actress Benno said to me: 'You act like an angel.'

Playwright Gosh! And fully recovered in twenty-four hours.

Actress You know nothing. The real reason I skipped the show was because I missed you so much!

Playwright I thought you did it to annoy me.

Actress You're so fucking shallow, do you know that? I had a temperature of 105. All because of you.

Playwright 105? That's quite a high temperature for a whim.

Actress A whim? I'm dying of love for you, and all you can call it is a whim.

The Playwright smiles and takes her in his arms.

Playwright And Fritz?

Actress Fuck Fritz. Oh, fuck, fuck Fritz.

The stage of the theatre, seen from the side. The sound of an ovation. The Actress is dressed for a performance of a play by Schnitzler. She lifts her arms to thank her public, the curtain comes down and she turns towards us. Her dressing room is full of flowers. There is a period chaise longue *at one side of the room, and a table with some Chinese takeaway on it. She goes out to the bathroom to start removing her costume. There is a nervous knock on the door and the Aristocrat comes in, thin and exquisite, in his early thirties. The Actress returns.*

Actress Good Lord . . .

Aristocrat I'm sorry . . .

Actress It's you.

Aristocrat The stage door-keeper suggested . . .

Actress Please come in.

Aristocrat It never occurred to me . . .

Actress Well, I am.

Aristocrat That you wouldn't have changed.

Actress Sit down.

The Aristocrat goes to perch nervously on the chaise longue.

Aristocrat You acted . . .

Actress Thank you.

Aristocrat Like an angel.

Actress It was something of a triumph, it seems.

Aristocrat *Something?* The audience were transported.

Actress Thank you for your flowers. (*She nods at the single huge bouquet of flowers.*) There they are.

Aristocrat Rather a small contribution, I'm afraid. You seem to be virtually buried by admirers.

The Actress looks at him a moment, then picks up all the flowers that are not his. She goes to the dressing room door, opens it, and throws them on to the floor in the corridor outside. She closes the door. Only his single vase of flowers remains.

Actress There. That's better isn't it? (*She reaches for his hand impulsively and puts it to her lips.*) Don't worry. It commits you to nothing.

The Aristocrat smiles.

Aristocrat People warned me you were completely unpredictable. Some people say, an enigma.

Actress I'm certainly more of an enigma than your little Bridget Cluny.

Aristocrat Well there's very little mystery in Bridget. (*He quickly corrects himself.*) Not that she's someone I know all that well.

Actress No?

Aristocrat Do you know I had never seen you act until tonight?

Actress Incredible.

Aristocrat The theatre's a big problem for me. Parking! And then eating so late.

73

Actress Why not eat before?

Aristocrat Yes, I've considered that. I don't like restaurants much at the best of times.

Actress What do you like?

Aristocrat It's a good question.

Actress You seem to me something of a young fuddy-duddy. (*She goes out to the bathroom.*)

Aristocrat Perhaps I just think too hard about things.

Actress (*off*) Oh, there's no point in thinking.

Aristocrat You're right. There is no point. People are people when it comes to it. I used to spend all my time thinking because I was bored. I was farming the family estate. Though at least in the country there are horses.

The Actress returns. She is wrapping herself in a big dressing gown, letting him glimpse her whalebone corset.

My God, why am I being so uninteresting?

Actress No, you're fascinating.

The Aristocrat smiles at her.

Aristocrat What about you? Are you fond of people?

Actress People? Lord, no. I can't stand them.

Aristocrat That's what I thought.

Actress I'm alone all the time. I'm virtually a recluse.

Aristocrat Of course.

Actress I see no one. No one!

Aristocrat That's inevitable. For an artist. But an artist is fortunate. Because the artist has a reason to live.

74

Actress What makes you think that?

Aristocrat Well . . .

Actress Me, I have nothing to live for! (*She has sat down at her dressing-room table and is taking off her wig.*)

Aristocrat But you're famous . . . everywhere you go you're praised . . .

Actress Praise? You think *praise* brings happiness? Please!

Aristocrat I didn't say happiness. That doesn't exist. Surely, isn't that what the play's saying?

Actress The play!

Aristocrat As I watched, I thought yes, this is true. This play says something true. When you fall in love, the feeling is there. It's real. It seems so real. Then, strange thing. It's gone.

Actress (*grandly*) It's gone!

Aristocrat Each time you look back, you think, 'From the start it was wrong. I should have known.' But how do we know? How do we ever know?

Actress Malcolm, you go to the very heart of things.

The Aristocrat shakes his head thoughtfully.

Aristocrat And so it scarcely matters – does it? – whether you're as grotesquely rich as I am, or mouse-poor. If you live in the town or in Timbuktu. For example . . . I've lost my umbrella. Oh, thank you . . . now where was I?

Actress Timbuktu.

Aristocrat Oh yes. I'm rambling. But my life is a search.

Actress A search?

Aristocrat Yes. For a love which stays real.

The Actress looks at him a moment.

Actress What are Miss Cluny's views on the subject?

Aristocrat What is this with Bridget?

Actress She is your girlfriend after all.

Aristocrat Is she?

Actress It says in the papers.

Aristocrat Perhaps somebody should have told me.

Actress Oh, Malcolm, come here! (*She laughs and pulls him towards her. She starts stroking his hair.*) I knew you were here tonight.

Aristocrat You knew? How?

Actress I spotted you.

Aristocrat What? From the stage?

Actress My whole performance was directed at you.

Aristocrat At me?

Actress Didn't you feel it? That diffidence of yours, your self-effacement . . .

Aristocrat I had no idea.

Actress It drives women nuts. And now kiss me at least . . .

The Aristocrat leans across and kisses her.

You are such a fake. Think how jealous every other man in the audience would be . . .

Aristocrat I know . . .

Actress Every night I feel them out there, pulsing, vibrating, like a physical force, all longing to rise up out of their

76

seats, clamber over the stalls, leap up on stage and have me on the boards . . .

Aristocrat Shall I tell you the truth? I'm frightened. (*He stops, in agony.*) Let me explain. We've been frank with one another. I've reached a point in my life. I want things to be right. I want things to be perfect. The beginning has to be right. If I'm honest, what I want is not to do it right now. (*He pauses.*) And to be truthful, I find love not in a bed rather distasteful. (*He hastens to explain.*) With most – as it were – women, what does it matter? But with someone like you it's important. Because we will always remember the first time. So . . . please . . .

Actress God, how adorable you are!

Aristocrat Let me tell you . . .

Actress How sweet!

Aristocrat What I propose . . .

Actress What do you propose?

Aristocrat Tomorrow, I collect you, we drive off, we book a hotel, somewhere out of town . . .

Actress I am not Bridget Cluny!

Aristocrat I didn't say you were. I am saying: listen, romance is important. Mood is important.

> *The Actress has got up and locked the dressing-room door. She turns off the lights.*

First, establish an atmosphere. And then . . .

Actress Yes? Then?

Aristocrat Go on from there.

Actress Sit closer. Come closer.

Aristocrat There's a scent. What is it? A scent from the *chaise longue*. Frangipani?

Actress It's so hot in here, don't you think?

The Aristocrat leans down and kisses her throat.

Aristocrat Yes, it's hot.

Actress And dark, also, don't you think? Dark as night. (*She draws him closer.*) Oh, Malcolm, are you sure? Is this the right start?

Music engulfs them. Darkness.

&

The light returns. He is fully dressed, sitting at the little table using chopsticks on her cold Chinese takeaway. She is lying back where we last saw her. They both look happy.

Actress So?

Aristocrat Well?

There is a silence. He eats.

Actress What was that about *mood*?

Aristocrat Hmm . . .

Actress I thought *mood* was meant to be important. I thought not-in-a-bed was beneath you.

Aristocrat You're a bitch.

Actress Thank you.

Aristocrat Not a bitch. A goddess.

Actress And I think you were born to be an actor. Truly. You understand women completely.

The Aristocrat stops eating a moment.

Aristocrat Do you think any of us is ever just one person? Don't you think we all change, all the time? With one person we're one person, and with another we're another.

Actress You think so?

Aristocrat I do. I'm quite a different person when I'm mucking out. (*He looks at her, then resumes eating.*)

Actress Do you know what I'm going to do now?

Aristocrat Do what?

Actress I'm going to tell you that I never want to see you ever again.

Aristocrat What are you saying?

Actress I'm out of my league. You're much too dangerous for me. You sit there as if nothing has happened. May I remind you: you've just debauched me.

Aristocrat (*smiles*) Can I ever forget it?

Actress And tomorrow?

Aristocrat What tomorrow?

Actress Are you . . .

Aristocrat What, see you?

Actress Going to see me?

Suddenly the Aristocrat raises his voice, provoked by the inevitability of it all.

Aristocrat What do we do? Tell me what we should do!

Actress What do you mean?

Aristocrat Don't we see already how this will unfold?

Actress No!

79

Aristocrat Aren't we on a track? Don't we say, 'Oh yes, this is the moment when *this*' and 'Oh Lord, here we go, here comes the moment when *that*!' Don't we *know* already?

Actress Even if you were right, what's that? A reason for not doing anything? What are you saying? Nothing's worth doing because nothing ends well?

The Aristocrat smiles, conceding.

Philosophy? Thank you. I get it from a book.

Aristocrat Books teach us nothing.

Actress Well then, there you are!

Aristocrat Nothing!

Actress You're right. Everything ends badly, because everyone dies! So, until then, what? This way, at least we're alive. Meet me tomorrow. Learn. It's the only way of learning.

They look at each other in silence.

Aristocrat I've stayed long enough. You have to act tomorrow.

Actress Not just tomorrow. Not just me.

There is a silence. The Aristocrat takes the key from her. He inclines his head very slightly.

Aristocrat It was a pleasure to see you.

Actress Mutual.

The Aristocrat goes to the door.

Aristocrat *Au revoir.*

Actress *Adieu*, Timbuktu.

10. THE ARISTOCRAT AND THE GIRL

At once the wail of a saxophone. Night streets, neon and alcohol. Dawn is breaking in a room above a sex shop in the centre of the town. Outside it is raining and a red sign advertising the shop is seen through a thin film of curtain. Inside the room, the Girl is asleep in a bed, her clothes thrown down all around her. On a leather chair at the other side of the room, the Aristocrat is lying, fully dressed. Beside him there is a near-empty bottle of tequila. After a moment or two, he stirs and looks round.

He is obviously hung-over and mystified by what he sees. He plainly has no memory of how he got here. He looks across to the Girl asleep in the bed.

Aristocrat Oh God, never again! I swore, never again! What did I do? Drink the whole day? (*He gets up, painfully. He rolls some words out to reassure himself he can speak.*) Amnesia. A medical term . . . for forgetting. Synaesthesia. A medical term . . . a medical term for experiencing sensation in a part of the body other than the one directly stimulated. (*He smiles, pleased at his success.*) The whole joke of life: you feel one thing but it comes out as another. Proust tastes the madeleine, but he sees the village. (*He suddenly calls out in what seems like genuine despair.*) Why do we do it? Why do we go on?

The Girl wakes at the noise of his questions.

Good morning.

Girl Hi, baby!

Aristocrat Did you sleep well?

Girl Mmm.

The Aristocrat moves towards her. A shaft of sunlight is falling on her face.

Aristocrat I was just off.

The Girl takes her hand out from under the blanket. She is tousled, warm. He shakes it, holding on a moment.

As if she were divine!

Girl What are you staring at?

Aristocrat Oh, the way the light is falling. The way you woke. (*He looks at her a moment.*) You're a pretty girl. You could easily find a man. (*He stops, serious.*) How old are you?

Girl Twenty in December.

Aristocrat And how long . . .

Girl A year.

Aristocrat A year. (*He takes out his wallet and removes a generous number of notes.*) I must go.

The Girl turns over to go back to sleep. The Aristocrat stops. The Girl's face is turned towards him, the sun stronger now, as on a mask.

May I ask you a favour? Please. Please don't say a word. (*He leans down and kisses her eyes.*) God, if you weren't . . . who you are, you could make your fortune.

Girl Yeah, that's what Fred says.

Aristocrat Fred? Who's Fred?

Girl Just a friend. He drives a cab.

Aristocrat And? (*He makes to go.*) Perhaps we'll meet again.

The Girl's eyes remain closed.

Girl Just ask for Irene.

Aristocrat Irene. Fair enough. (*He stops once more at the door.*) Still, it's something, eh? I've spent the whole night with her and all I've done is kiss her eyes. That's something. (*He smiles, pleased with himself.*) Irene, does this happen a lot?

Girl What?

Aristocrat That men leave you. That they just leave you?

Girl Sure. Every day.

Aristocrat No, I mean without . . . without . . .

Girl No. Never!

Aristocrat But . . .

Girl Of course not!

Aristocrat It doesn't mean I don't like you.

Girl I know that. You liked me well enough last night.

The Aristocrat frowns.

Aristocrat I like you now.

Girl Yes, but you liked me better last night.

The light is growing at the window, circling the Girl with yellow.

Don't tell me you've forgotten.

Aristocrat Yes. No.

Girl Then afterwards you fell asleep.

Aristocrat Yes. I do that. That's what I did, then.

There is a silence. The Girl is quite still and her tone is kind.

Girl God, you must have been drunk, baby.

Aristocrat Yes.

The Girl turns over to go to sleep. He stands at the door.

Well . . . it would have been romantic if I'd just kissed her eyes. That would have been romantic. But there we are. It wasn't to be. On we go.

In the distance, the day is starting. The town is coming to life and the saxophone is beginning to play again. The Girl stands up and sleepily drags her bed across the room. They look at one another for a moment.

Goodnight.

Girl Good morning.

Aristocrat Yes, of course. Good morning. Good morning.

The music grows louder. He stands, not moving. Then he turns decisively and goes. The stage begins to close down and darken. Then we are completely shut out.